THE LITTLE MATCHGIRL

RETOLD FROM THE ORIGINAL BY HANS CHRISTIAN ANDERSEN

Once upon a time, there lived a little girl who was so frail that she looked as if the slightest gust of wind might blow her away. The poor little girl was clothed in the thinnest rags and spent all her days and nights wandering the streets trying to sell matches.

"Matches, who'll buy my matches?" cried the little girl over and over again, but nobody was interested. A wealthy merchant, with arms full of parcels bustled past the sad little creature. "Out of my way," he shouted, knocking her tray of matches all over the pavement. But he wasn't sorry for what he'd done. His mind was on the big juicy goose that his servants were cooking for his supper.

Oh what a pathetic little figure the little matchgirl looked as she stooped to pick up the matches. And as all the healthy and wealthy people of the city rushed past her, not one of them even offered to help. They were far too busy with their own lives for that.

Soon the streets were full of mothers walking home with their children. All the children chattered happily, because their mothers had bought them lovely presents.

How the little matchgirl's heart ached to make friends with one of the children. Oh how she would have loved to be invited into their warm and happy homes. But it was not to be. They hadn't even noticed her. She was so busy staring at the children that she didn't see a carriage driving past at full speed. It was only when she heard the angry shouts of the driver that she managed to leap out of the way.

The little matchgirl had leapt out of the way of the carriage so quickly, that she had lost one of her slippers. And before she had the chance to pick it up, a street urchin found it and wouldn't give it back to her.

"Don't you try and catch me, I'm going to keep this slipper and use it as a doll's cradle,"shouted the little rascal as he disappeared into the crowds. "Stop him, stop him somebody,"she shouted. But nobody was listening to her.

This was the last straw for the little matchgirl. She was far too tired and hungry to chase after him, so she knelt down and started to cry. "What am I to do?" she sobbed. "I'm cold and hungry and all alone in the world. Please, somebody help me." And the poor little creature was so cold that the tears froze as they rolled down her cheeks.

"Matches, who'll buy my matches?" she cried over and over again, but her voice was getting much weaker, and she could barely be heard above the sound of the children chattering.

There was no point in her returning home that night, because she hadn't sold a single match all day. She knew her mother and father would beat her if she returned home without any money. So she wandered the streets as the snow fell heavily on her poor little body.

As she walked by all the large and beautiful houses in the city, she noticed that all their windows were lit up. And as she peered inside each house she saw much happiness and feasting and longed to be a part of it all. In one house she saw the wealthy merchant carving his goose, in another she heard gasps of excitement from children as they opened their presents. In another she saw a handsome man playing the piano. The guests were elegantly dressed, and clapped enthusiastically when the pianist had finished his performance. The little matchgirl pressed her face closer to the window to get a better look but as she did this a stern looking man drew the curtains in one quick sweep.

So the little matchgirl found herself alone once again on this night of all nights - Christmas Eve. By now, the snow was falling so heavily that the little matchgirl sheltered in one of the doorways of the grand houses. She knew that the only way to keep warm was to light one of her precious matches."Should I light one?" she whispered. "My mother and father would certainly beat me if they found out that I was using the matches myself."

She thought about it for a while and then she saw a stray dog who was sitting nearby. The poor little creature looked as cold and lonely as she felt. "What shall I do, little dog?"said the little matchgirl. "Do you think I should light a match to keep myself warm?" The dog gave out a little bark and she took this to mean "Yes".

So the little matchgirl took a match from her apron and struck it against the wall of the house. How warm she felt as the little flame burned in front of her eyes. She held her hand around it, so that it didn't go out straightaway.

Suddenly the little flame turned into a big metal stove and on the stove sat a piping hot pot of tea. And as the little girl stretched out her arms to pour herself a cup, the stove disappeared and she was left, alone once again with nothing but a burned out match for company.

Desperate to feel warm again, she struck another match against the wall of the house. The flame lit up the wall and within seconds, it was as if the wall had become transparent, because she could see into one of the grand rooms of the house. Oh what a magnificent feast had appeared before her very eyes. She saw a table that looked even grander than the wealthy merchant's table.

The finest glasses and china were set upon a beautiful cotton tablecloth and right in the middle of the table sat the juiciest, most enormous goose she had ever seen. "Mmmm, how heavenly the goose smells," whispered the little matchgirl.

The sad little girl then licked her lips at the thought of tasting the delicious fare. But what happened next was truly amazing. The goose, although it had a huge knife and fork stuck in its back, started waddling towards her. "Let me touch you," she said, but as soon as she said this the flame went out, and she was left touching the cold stone walls of the house.

Hoping to see more beautiful things, she lit a third match. This time, the little flame, turned into a wonderful Christmas tree. It was even more special than the Christmas tree that stood in the city square every year - and that was very special indeed.

Many baubles and candles were fixed on the dark green branches of this magical Christmas tree. The little matchgirl tried to count all the candles...one...two...three ...four...five...six...seven... eight...nine...but by the time she'd got to ten, the tree and all its candles had vanished and once again she was left with a burned out match.

"Come back, beautiful tree," she cried and as she looked up into the sky, she saw that the candles of the Christmas tree had turned into hundreds of shining stars.

The little matchgirl reached out to try and touch the stars, and as she did this, a shooting star flew across the sky and landed in her hands. It gave her hands a warm, tingling feeling - it was a magical feeling, quite unlike anything she'd ever felt before. Suddenly she felt full of hope and happiness.

She looked on in amazement as the star shot out of her hands and back across the sky. She didn't let it out of her sight until its fiery tail had faded into the distance. Even the matches leapt out of her hands and seemed to dance with delight. And then she remembered the night when she and her grandmother had watched a shooting star light up the sky. "When you see a shooting star, it means a soul is returning to heaven," her grandmother had told her.

She started thinking about her grandmother, who had died a few years ago. The little matchgirl felt happy and sad at the same time when she remembered that her grandmother had been the only person who had ever shown her any kindness.

To warm herself up, she lit another match, and as its little flame flickered her kind and lovely grandmother appeared. She looked happier and lovelier than she had ever looked before."Dear grandmother," shouted the little girl, "how I've missed you. Take me with you before you disappear. The stove, goose and Christmas tree may have only paid me a brief visit, but I want to stay with you for ever and ever."

She then struck all the other matches she had left in quick succession, in the hope that her grandmother would stay.

The flames from all the matches burned so bright, that they lit up the whole sky. In fact it seemed as if night had turned into day.

"How beautiful you look tonight," said the little matchgirl as she looked at her grandmother.

And as the little matchgirl reached out to touch her, her grandmother lifted her up and flew away with her.

"Tonight we are going to Paradise, little one. It is a place where you will never feel cold or hungry again," her grandmother said. So over the snowy rooftops of the grand houses and the tree tops they flew, until they were so high in the sky that the houses looked like little dolls' houses and the trees looked as if they were matchsticks.

The next morning, the little matchgirl was found on the cold, snow-covered street. She had a glow in her cheeks and she looked as if she was asleep. An old man took off his coat to wrap around her and he shook her arm gently to wake her. But the little girl was dead.

"The poor little thing had been trying to warm herself," cried the old man when he saw the burned out matches by her side. And as a crowd gathered, many people shed tears for her. But little did they know that she had seen the most wonderful visions and that she had gone to a place where she would never feel cold again.